NEW YEAR
Around the World

Elspeth Graham

OXFORD
UNIV

OXFORD
UNIVERSITY PRESS

Great Clarendon Street, Oxford OX2 6DP

Oxford University Press is a department of the University of Oxford.
It furthers the University's objective of excellence in research, scholarship,
and education by publishing worldwide in

Oxford New York

Athens Auckland Bangkok Bogotá Buenos Aires Calcutta
Cape Town Chennai Dar es Salaam Delhi Florence Hong Kong Istanbul
Karachi Kuala Lumpur Madrid Melbourne Mexico City Mumbai
Nairobi Paris São Paulo Singapore Taipei Tokyo Toronto Warsaw

with associated companies in Berlin Ibadan

Oxford is a registered trade mark of Oxford University Press
in the UK and in certain other countries

Published in the United Kingdom
by Oxford University Press

Text © Elspeth Graham 2000

British Library Cataloguing in Publication Data

Data available

ISBN 0 19 915701 4

Available in packs
Celebrations   Pack of Six (one of each book)   ISBN 0 19 915703 0
Celebrations   Class Pack (six of each book)   ISBN 0 19 915704 9

Printed in Hong Kong

Acknowledgements

The Publisher would like to thank the following for permission
to reproduce photographs:

Asiafoto: p 18; J Allan Cash: p 17; Circa Photo Library/John Smith: p 12;
Corbis UK Ltd/Richard Bickel: p 20; Corbis UK Ltd/Natalie Fobes: p 14; Corbis
UK Ltd/Kelly Mooney Photography: p 23 (top); Corbis UK Ltd/Neil Rabinowitz:
p 22 (bottom); The Robert Harding Picture Library/Jeff Greenburg: p 23
(bottom); The Hutchison Library: p 7; The Hutchison Library/Trevor Page: p 9;
The Hutchison Library/Edward Parker: p 6; Ann & Bury Peerless: p 13 (top);
Tony Stone Images/Nadia Mackenzie: p 13 (bottom); Telegraph Colour Library/
Jeffrey Aaronson: p 22 (top).

Front cover photographs are by Corel Professional Photos (top) and Ann &
Bury Peerless (bottom).

Illustrations by Tony Morris c/o Linda Rogers Artists, Yvonne Muller,
Viv Quillin, and Martin Sanders.

Contents

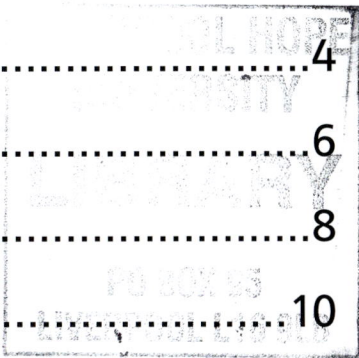

Introduction

The beginning of a year is a time for hope and change. It is a time of magic and legends.

People celebrate a new year in different ways around the world. Some welcome the new year with prayer. Others welcome the new year with fire, water, flowers or dancing.

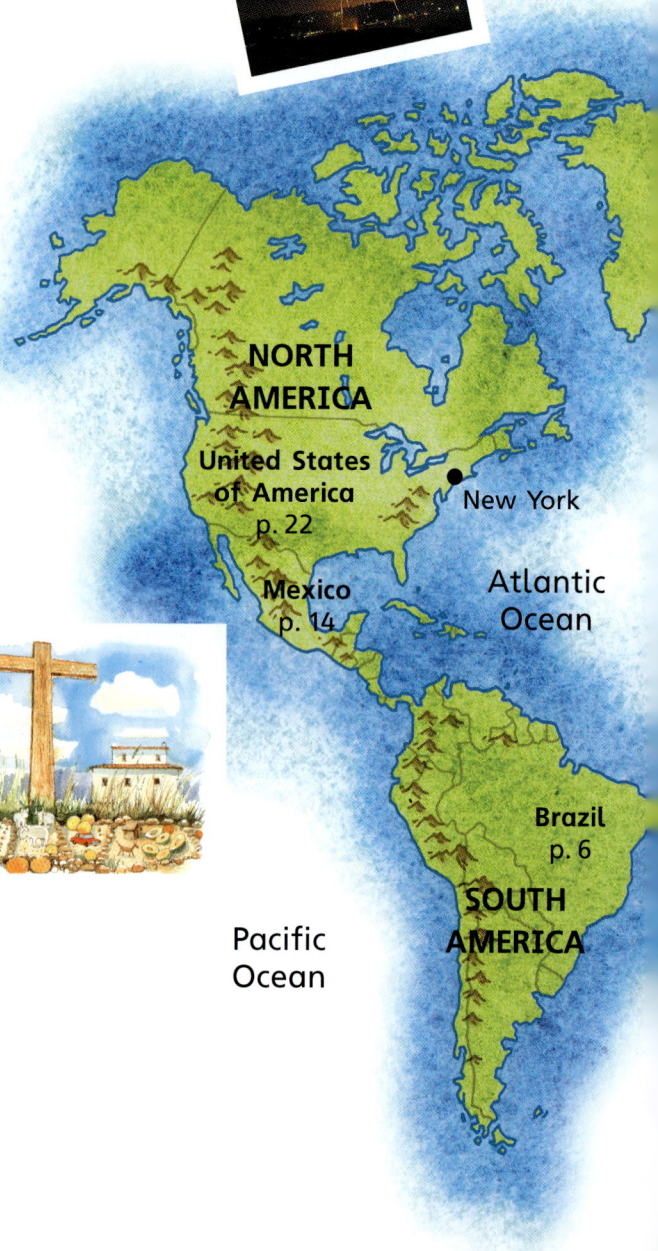

NORTH
AMERICA

United States
of America
p. 22

New York

Mexico
p. 14

Atlantic
Ocean

Brazil
p. 6

SOUTH
AMERICA

Pacific
Ocean

Around the world

This world map shows the places which appear in the rest of the book. Look back at it while you are reading, to see where the people live.

Arctic Ocean

Shetland
Islands
p. 17

Scotland
p. 16

EUROPE

ASIA

Greece
p. 10

China
p. 8

India
p. 12

AFRICA

Thailand
p. 20

Indian
Ocean

Pacific
Ocean

Indonesia

AUSTRALASIA

Island of
Sumba
p. 18

Australia
p. 9

Southern Ocean

Brazil

In Brazil, the eve of the new year is the special day of Yermanja, the goddess of the sea. Yermanja controls storms, so people pray to her for a safe journey if they are travelling by sea.

People believe that Yermanja is the mother of all other gods and goddesses in their religion.

Along the coast, people gather at the beach for parties. They light candles and set off fireworks. They play music and sing to the goddess.

Then people wade into the sea and lay flowers on the water. If the flowers are washed out to sea, the next year will bring good luck.

White flowers are offered to Yermanja because white is one of her favourite colours.

China

A Chinese **legend** says that a wicked monster comes down from the mountains at the end of the old year. The monster is scared of loud noises, bright lights, and the colour red, so Chinese people use all these things to scare it away.

Fireworks are set off. Children are given gifts of money in special red envelopes. Good luck rhymes are written on red paper and stuck on doors.

The Dragon dance

In the streets, gongs crash and drums beat. Dancers dress up as animals. Lions, monkeys, cats and roosters roll and leap into the air.

New Year is celebrated by Chinese people living all over the world.

Dragons dance at the front of the procession. They are sometimes led with a lantern or a "pearl".

One of the longest dragons in the world is in Perth, Australia. It is 56m from nose to tail.

Greece

In Greece, New Year's Day is the festival of Saint Basil. Saint Basil is known for his kindness to children.

Children leave their shoes out on New Year's Eve for Saint Basil to fill with gifts. ▶

Families make a special cake with a ring or gold coin hidden in it.

▲ Whoever finds the ring or coin in their piece of cake is supposed to have a lucky year.

On some Greek islands, children go from house to house with a model of Saint Basil's ship. The little ship is painted gold. The children beat small drums, play triangles, and sing songs.

When the children have finished their singing and playing, people give them sweets, figs, or money.

Mexico

In many parts of Mexico, New Year's Eve is celebrated with carnivals. Streets are decorated with streamers and flowers. There is music and dancing. At night there are firework displays.

Piñatas

Clay or paper models called "piñatas" are hung up. Blindfolded children try to break the piñata with a stick.

The piñata is full of sweets or water.

Wishing Night

In the Mexican village of Mitla, New Year's Eve is called "Wishing Night". The villagers gather around a cross just outside the village. They make wishes for the coming year.

The villagers make tiny models to show their wishes and lay them around the cross.

Scotland

In Scotland, New Year is called "Hogmanay".
The first visitor to a house after midnight is
called a "first-footer". He or she can bring
good luck for the year ahead. The best luck
comes with a tall, dark man.

I think you'd better go first

If he brings coal with him the
family will keep warm. If he brings
bread they will not be hungry.

Up-Helly-Aa

The Shetland Islands are part of Scotland. The people who live there are descended from Vikings. At New Year, they have a fire festival called Up-Helly-Aa.

Some men dress up as Vikings, with cloaks and winged helmets. They parade with blazing torches.

At the end of the festival they set fire to a great Viking ship with a dragon's head and tail.

Sumba

Every year, millions of brightly-coloured worms appear on the beaches of Sumba in Indonesia. When they come, the new year begins.

The worms come to the island of Sumba in February or March.

Priests use the worms to tell the future. If the worms nip when they are picked up, the year will bring bad luck. If the worms are peaceful, the year will be good.

After the worms have shown the future, the people of Sumba have a pretend battle. One hundred horsemen fight each other. People believe that the battle will help crops to grow and children to be born.

The horsemen use blunt wooden swords and spears so that no-one gets hurt.

Thailand

In Thailand, the temple bells ring 108 times at midnight on the eve of a new year. One hundred and eight is a special number which is supposed to bring good luck.

Statues of **Buddha** are washed with scented water. People throw coloured and scented water over each other, and have lots of fun with hosepipes.

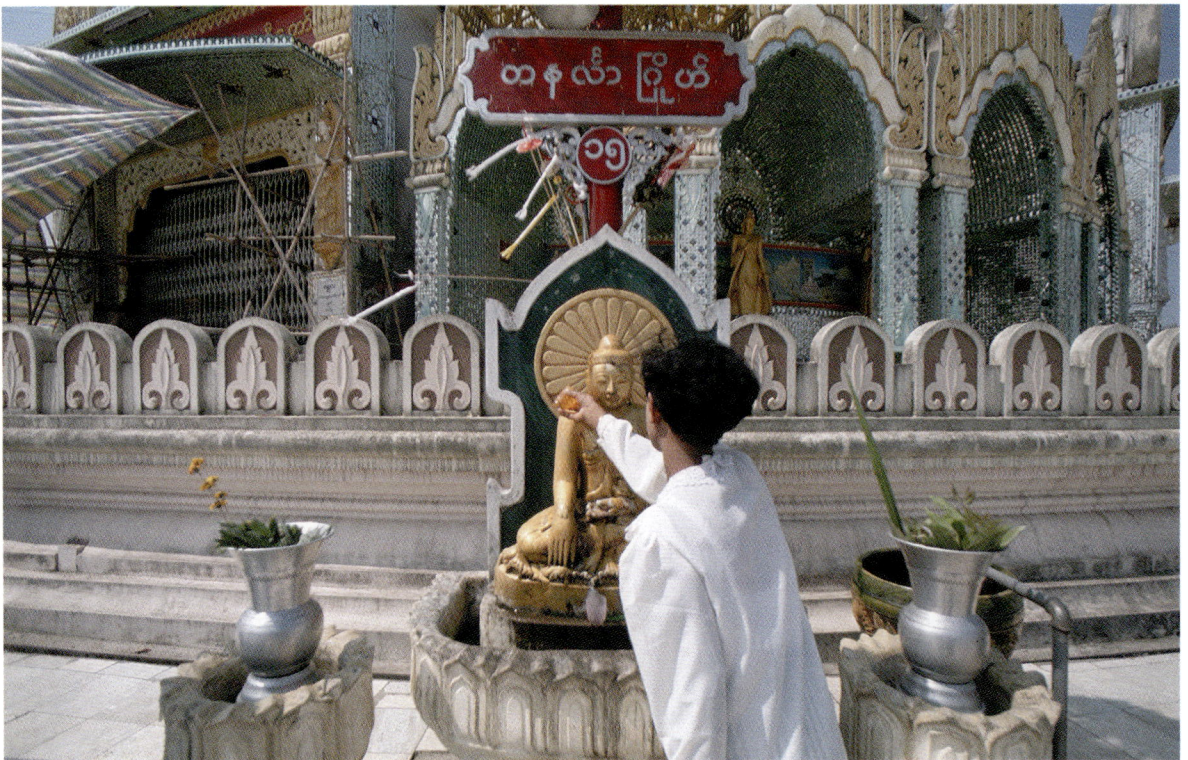

▲ **Buddhists** wash statues of Buddha as a sign that they are ready for a fresh start.

A kind deed for a new year

People in Thailand believe that a kind deed at the beginning of the new year will bring good luck. They sometimes buy fish or caged birds and set them free on New Year's Day.

Some people buy turtles to set free. This turtle has been decorated with gold paper for extra good luck.

United States of America

There are many New Year's Day celebrations in the United States of America.

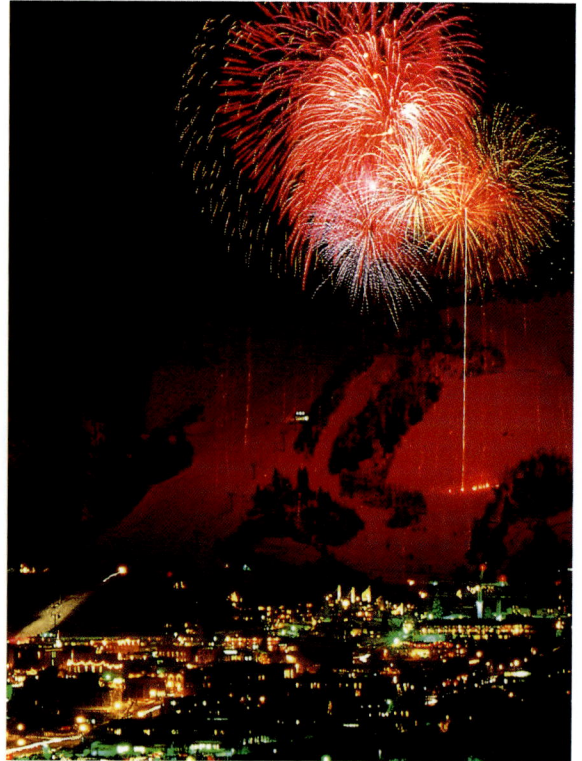

At Pikes Peak in Colorado there is a great firework display. Many people watch the sky burst into colour at New Year.

The **Tournament** of the Roses takes place in Pasadena, California. Millions of flowers are used to cover **floats** that parade through the streets.

Midnight in Times Square

In New York City, thousands of people fill Times Square on New Year's Eve. They have a huge outdoor party to welcome the new year. They count down the seconds to midnight.

America is so big that the time at the east coast is three hours ahead of the time at the west coast. People in California can turn on their television at 9 p.m. on New Year's Eve and watch the midnight celebrations in New York.

5... 4... 3... 2... 1... Happy New Year!

Times Square on New Year's Eve ▶

23

Glossary

526504

Buddha An Indian prince who became a great teacher. His name means "the awakened one".

Buddhists People who follow the teachings of Buddha.

floats Trucks or trailers decorated for a parade.

Hindu A person who follows the main religion in India, Hinduism.

legend A story from long, long ago.

tournament A contest.

Index

£2.99   9/2000